Patriotic Songs

America
the
Beautiful

A Song to Celebrate the Wonders of America

Written by Katharine Lee Bates
Edited by Ann Owen • Illustrated by Todd Ouren

Music Adviser: Peter Mercer-Taylor, Ph.D.
Associate Professor of Musicology, University of Minnesota, Minneapolis

Reading Adviser: Susan Kesselring, M.A., Literacy Educator
Rosemount-Apple Valley-Eagan (Minnesota) School District

PICTURE WINDOW BOOKS
Minneapolis, Minnesota

Patriotic Songs series editor: Sara E. Hoffmann
Musical arrangement: Elizabeth Temple
Designer: John Moldstad
Page production: Picture Window Books
The illustrations in this book were prepared digitally.

Printed in the United States of America.
1 2 3 4 5 6 08 07 06 05 04 03

Picture Window Books
5115 Excelsior Boulevard
Suite 232
Minneapolis, MN 55416
1-877-845-8392
www.picturewindowbooks.com

Library of Congress Cataloging-in-Publication Data
Bates, Katharine Lee, 1859-1929.
America the beautiful / written by Katharine Lee Bates ;
edited by Ann Owen ; illustrated by Todd Ouren.
p. cm. — (Patriotic songs)
Summary: Provides a history and words to four verses of the song, "America
the Beautiful," as well as simple instructions for making a patriotic garden.
ISBN 1-4048-0172-3 (library binding)
1. Bates, Katharine Lee, 1859-1929—Juvenile literature. 2. National songs—
United States—History and criticism—Juvenile literature. 3. Patriotic music—
United States—History and criticism—Juvenile literature. [1. Patriotic music. 2.
Songs. 3. Bates, Katharine Lee, 1859-1929.] I. Owen, Ann, 1953-
II. Ouren, Todd, ill. III. Title. IV. Series.
ML3551 .B26 2003
782.42'1599'0973—dc21
                                                    2002154686

O say, can you hear America singing?
America's patriotic songs are a record of the country's history.
Many of these songs were written when the United States was young.
Some songs were inspired by war and some by thoughts of peace and freedom.
They all reflect the country's spirit and dreams.

O beautiful for patriot dream that sees beyond the years.

O beautiful for spacious skies,

5

for amber waves of grain,

for purple mountain majesties

above the fruited plain.

10

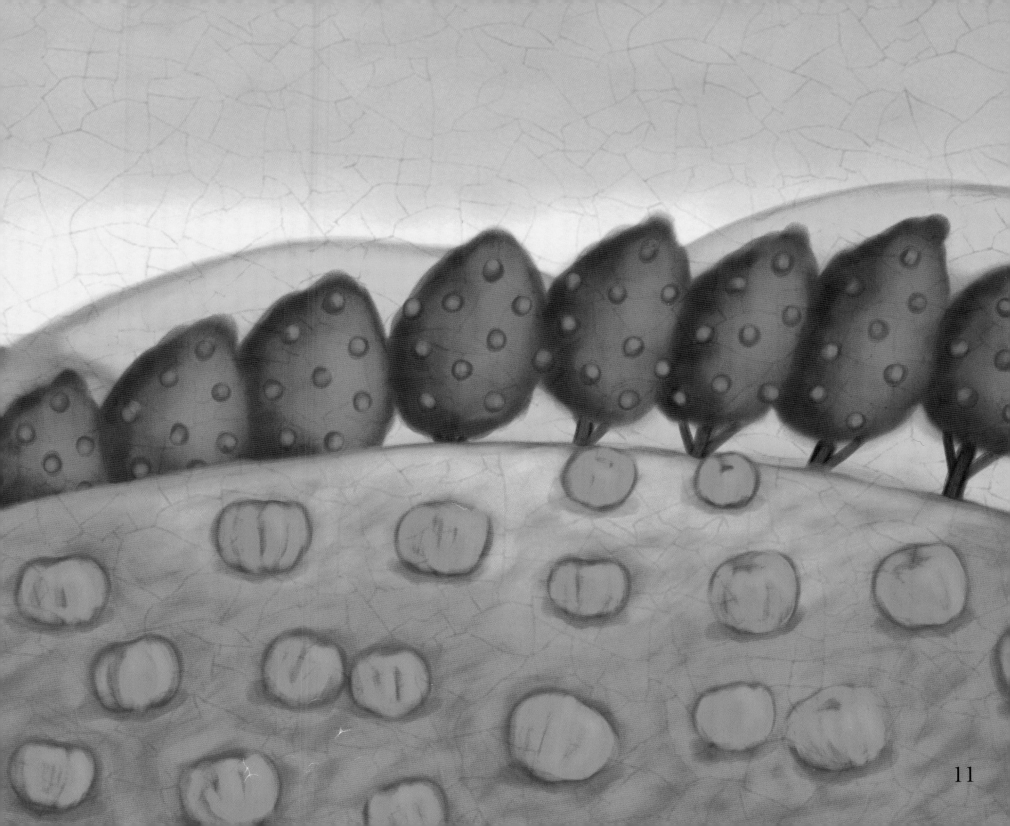

11

America! America!
God shed His grace on thee,

and crown thy good with brotherhood

from sea to shining sea.

15

O beautiful for patriot dream

that sees beyond the years.

17

Thine alabaster cities gleam, undimmed by human tears.

America! America!
God shed His grace on thee,

and crown thy good with brotherhood

from sea to shining sea.

America the Beautiful

O beau - ti - ful for spa - cious skies, for am - ber waves of grain, for pur - ple moun - tain ma - jes-ties a - bove the frui - ted plain. A - me - ri - ca! A - me - ri - ca! God shed His grace on thee, and crown thy good with bro - ther - hood from sea to shi - ning sea.

O beautiful for pilgrims' feet,
Whose stern impassioned stress,
A thoroughfare for freedom beat
Across the wilderness.
America! America!
God mend thine every flaw,
Confirm thy soul in self-control,
Thy liberty in law.

O beautiful for heroes proved
In liberating strife,
Who more than self their country loved,
And mercy more than life.
America! America!
May God thy gold refine,
Till all success be nobleness
And every gain divine.

O beautiful for patriot dream
That sees beyond the years
Thine alabaster cities gleam
Undimmed by human tears.
America! America!
God shed His grace on thee,
And crown thy good with brotherhood
From sea to shining sea.

About the Song

Katharine Lee Bates was a young college professor in 1893. That year, she traveled from her home in Massachusetts to teach at a summer program in Colorado. Along the way she stopped at the World's Columbian Exposition. At this huge fair, people could see the newest inventions of the time, including zippers and electric lights. The displays were inside buildings made of gleaming white plaster—an alabaster city, thought the young professor.

Katharine saw many beautiful sights on her trip west. Later that summer, she joined a group that traveled by wagon up Pike's Peak in Colorado. After a slow, bumpy ride up the mountain, the group reached the top. Katharine was amazed by the lovely view. That night she began working on the poem that would become "America the Beautiful."

The poem was first published two years later. Katharine changed it twice, once in 1904 and again in 1913. Since then, there have been many different musical arrangements of the poem. The most popular one uses the tune from a hymn written by Samuel A. Ward.

Did you know?

To celebrate the 1893 Columbian Exposition, Francis J. Bellamy, the editor of a popular children's magazine, *Youth's Companion*, wrote "The Salute to the Flag," which we now call "The Pledge of Allegiance."

You Can Make a Patriotic Garden

What you need:

Clay flower pot

Red, white, and blue acrylic paints

Brushes

Cardboard

Scissors

Aluminum foil

Glue or tape

Craft sticks

Modeling clay or Styrofoam

What to do:

1. Paint the clay pot with stars and stripes, or any design in red, white, and blue.

2. While the paint dries, draw a star on the cardboard. Cut it out and use it to trace several other cardboard stars—as many as you want to plant in your pot.

3. Cut them all out and then cover each star with aluminum foil.

4. Tape or glue each star to a craft stick.

5. When the paint is dry on the pot, place some modeling clay or a piece of Styrofoam in the pot; this will hold the craft sticks.

6. Now you can plant your stars.

To Learn More

At the Library

Bates, Katharine Lee. *America the Beautiful*. New York: Aladdin Paperbacks, 2002.

Guthrie, Woody. *This Land Is Your Land*. Boston: Little, Brown, 1998.

Loomis, Christine. *Across America, I Love You*. New York: Hyperion Books for Children, 2000.

Raatma, Lucia. *Patriotism*. Mankato, Minn.: Bridgestone Books, 2000.

Younger, Barbara. *Purple Mountain Majesties: The Story of Katharine Lee Bates and "America The Beautiful"*. New York: Dutton Children's Books, 1998.

On the Web

FirstGov for Kids

http://www.kids.gov

For fun links and information about the United States and its government

National Institute of Environmental Health Sciences Kids' Page: Patriotic Songs

http://www.niehs.nih.gov/kids/musicpatriot.htm

For lyrics and music to your favorite patriotic songs

Want to learn more about patriotic songs?
Visit FACT HOUND at http://www.facthound.com.